Dearest Dorothy

with love from

Millie

"Happy Birthday"

Oct. 6, 1966

Cherry-Blossoms

JAPANESE HAIKU

SERIES III

TRANSLATIONS OF
POEMS BY BASHO ·
BUSON · ISSA · SHIKI
AND OTHERS

THE PETER
PAUPER PRESS

MOUNT VERNON · NEW YORK

A NOTE ON THIS BOOK OF HAIKU

IN JAPAN cherry-blossoms are a favorite subject of paintings and poems, and are indeed a symbol to the Japanese people of the transitory delight of the "floating world" — as they have called this life on earth. For cherry-blossoms last only three days, and the Buddhist Japanese thinks of his own life as an equally brief flowering in the endless cycle of reincarnation and dissolution.

Because the *haiku* is a poem only seventeen syllables long, and is usually a brief poignant insight into the universality of this endless cycle, the title *Cherry-Blossoms* has been given to this our third collection of *haiku* translations.

Japanese poets of the present continue to write *haiku*: Harold G. Henderson has estimated that perhaps a million new *haiku* are published commercially in magazines each year. But the present collection is taken from the famous poets of the past. Thus the reader will find the names Basho, Buson, Issa and Shiki much in evidence, for these four are the greatest practitioners. A few facts about these men, and a discussion of the difficulties of *haiku* translation, are to be found in our two previous collections.

Here it is necessary only to remind the reader that the poems are not intended to be clear statements. They are fleeting responses or impressions which usually illuminate the poet's awareness — and our own — of the identity of life on different planes. It is the Buddhist doctrine (and most of these poets are Zen Buddhists) that all things and creatures in this world are temporary manifestations risen from the eternal, infinite ocean of Life; and that everything, — from a mountain peak to a cherry-blossom, from a beautiful girl to the little excrement of a bird, — is a part of the universal and inter-related brotherhood of creation.

Of course, not all these poems have this subtle quality. There are a number purely humorous or descriptive.

The *haiku* almost always has a season keyword. Here these have often been omitted, but the poems are arranged by seasons. Since the New Year traditionally begins the Spring, a few cold poems start the book; but the snow soon melts and leaves and blossoms appear.

The interested reader is referred to our *Japanese Haiku*: Series I, to *The Four Seasons*, Haiku Series II, and *Haiku Harvest*, Series IV.

Cherry-Blossoms

DECORATIONS AND
LETTERING BY
JEFF HILL

Spring

NEW YEAR'S EVE
I CAN SNORE IN PEACE . . .
    THE NEW YEAR
      WON'T CONFRONT ME
TILL TOMORROW NOON
               BUSON

NEW YEAR'S DAY . . . POET
    THOUGH I BE
      I'LL PROUDLY WEAR
MY FATHER'S SCABBARD
              KYORAI

IN THE NEW YEAR DAWN
    SOLEMN AND
      DELIBERATE
TALL CRANES GO MARCHING
             KIKAKU

FROM THE MOUNTAIN PASS
   SEE THE SUNLIT
   CASTLE TOWN . . .
FLYING NEW-YEAR KITES
            TAIGI

SEEING MY BIRTH-CORD
   KEPT AT OUR OLD
   NATIVE PLACE . . .
NEW YEAR'S DAY I WEPT
            BASHO

NO YOU DON'T! GET OUT! . . .
   THUS THEY WARMLY
   WELCOMED ME
TO THEIR NEW-YEAR FEAST
            ROTSU

SNOW IS MELTING . . .
   FAR IN THE MISTED
   MOUNTAINS
A CAW-CAWING CROW
            GYODAI

SPRING AT EARLY DAWN...
  ON THE TIPS OF
  BARLEY LEAVES
LITTLE LAST PALE FROST
                    ONITSURA

UP FROM APRIL SNOW
  RISING UDO SPROUTS...
  TENDER
PURPLE SUCCULENT
                      BASHO

AT DEAR BASHO'S GRAVE
  PALE THIN TRANSIENTS
  WE PAUSE...
SPRING MIST, SAD PUPIL
                      JOSO

HEAR THOSE BABY MICE
  HUDDLED IN THEIR
  NEST...PEEPING
TO THE SPARROWLETS
                      BASHO

8

ABOVE THE HAMLET:
   GREEN THE SILENT
   BAMBOO-GROVE...
WHITE LINGERING SNOW
                 TAIGI

SPRING COBALT OCEAN...
   ACROSS SNOW-WHITE
   MOUNTAINS FLY
BLACK RETURNING BIRDS
                 SHIKI

IMMEDIATELY...
   ON THEIR SPRING
   RETURN TIRELESS
SWALLOWS ZIG-ZAGGING
                 TAIGI

SEE: OUR CANDLELIGHT
   ILLUMINATES
   THE SAPLING'S
FRESH-UNFOLDED GOLD
                 BUSON

9

TROOPS OF TOURISTS COME
    FOR APRIL
    FLOWER-VIEWING...
OH, THEY'RE SPARROW-MEN
          BASHO

GUSTY SPRING BREEZES...
    BUT THE STUBBORN
    PLUM BUDS STILL
GRIPPING THEIR THIN TWIGS
          ONITSURA

SPRING UNFOLDS ANEW...
    NOW IN MY SECOND
    CHILDHOOD
FOLLY, FOLLY, TOO
          ISSA

BONY BRUSHWOOD TWIGS
    CUT DOWN AND STACKED
    IN BUNCHES...
YET BRAVELY BUDDING
          BONCHO

PLACING THE KITTEN
  TO WEIGH HER
    ON THE BALANCE ...
SHE WENT ON PLAYING
            ISSA

SPRING EVENING BEACH ...
  HELPING FISHERMEN
    UNLOAD
LIVING SEA-TREASURE
            RANKO

IT IS SPRING AGAIN ...
  GAY IN THE GARDEN
    GATHER
SUN-BATHING SPARROWS
            ONITSURA

TREMENDOUS FORCES ...
  STONE-PILED FENCE
    ALL TUMBLED DOWN
BY TWO CATS IN LOVE
            SHIKI

AFTER THE SHOWER...
   SPRING-ENCHANTED
   SPARROW-FOLK
CHATTER IN THE LEAVES
              UKO

SILENT CHERRY-BLOOM...
   AGAIN WITH YOUR
   OLD ELOQUENCE
ADDRESS MY INNER EAR
            ONITSURA

HAVING SCOURED MY SKIN
   AND BOWED MY SKULL
   TO BUDDHA...
NOW FOR CHERRY-BLOOM!
            ISSA

AFTERNOON GARDENS...
   PLANTING PERHAPS
   SEVEN SEEDS...
I'M CONVALESCENT!
            SHIKI

12

THIS BABY...EVEN
   WHEN WE SHOW HIM
   CHERRY BUDS...
OPENS EAGER LIPS
             SEIFU-JO

MOUNTAIN-TOP OF CLOUDS
   TOWERING BEHIND
   THE HEDGE...
OR A FLOWERING PLUM?
             SHIRO

DANCING: THE FOX TREADS
   AMONG THE PALE
   NARCISSI
IN GARDEN MOONLIGHT
             BUSON

AFTER SPRING SUNSET
   MIST RISES FROM
   THE RIVER...
SPREADING LIKE A FLOOD
             CHORA

13

THEN THE PEONIES
   EXTINGUISHING
   ALL OTHERS . . .
OPENED THEIR PETALS
              KIICHI

ENDLESS MAYTIME RAIN . . .
   SNEAKING BACK ONE
   NIGHT, THE MOON
PERCHED IN THE PINE-TREE
              RANKO

NOW THAT I AM OLD
   EVEN TENDER DAYS
   OF SPRING
SEE . . . CAN MAKE ME CRY
              ISSA

BEAUTIFUL LADY
   BUFFETED BY RUDE
   SPRING WINDS . . . WHAT
SWEET STORM YOU MAKE!
              KITO

ON THE SHINING ROOF
    THE BOY'S ABANDONED
    STRING-BALL
SOAKING UP SPRING RAIN
          BUSON

SWEET SPRING SHOWER ...
    ENOUGH TO WET
    THE TINY SHELLS
ON THIS LITTLE BEACH
          BUSON

ERE SPRING GUESTS ARRIVE
    WE LIGHT THE
    SUPPER CANDLES
EACH FROM SHINING EACH
          BUSON

DULL-DREARY RAIN-DAY ...
    DRIPPING PAST
    MY GATE A GIRL
BEARING IRISES
          SHINTOKU

YES: THE YOUNG SPARROWS
    IF YOU TREAT THEM
    TENDERLY...
THANK YOU WITH DROPPINGS
                                ISSA

FOLLOWING THE BANK...
    FOR MILES NO RIVER-
    SPANNING BRIDGE
THIS LONG SPRING DAY
                                SHIKI

AT TAKIGUCHI
    VOICES CALLING
    FOR A LIGHT...
DARKENING SPRING RAIN
                                BUSON

PATTERING SHOWER...
    THEY ARE PUTTING
    OUT THE LAMPS
ALL DOWN DOLL-SHOP LANE
                                BUSON

16

FLOODED PADDY-FIELDS...
   THE LAKE HAS COME
    TO TOWN ALL GREEN
WITH SEEDLING RICE
BAKUSUI

VANISHING SPRINGTIME...
   WISTFULLY
    THE LONELY WIDOW
POUTS AT HER MIRROR
SEIBI

BLOWN CHERRY-BLOSSOMS
   FALL AND FLOAT
    UPON THE COLD
RICE-PADDY WATERS
KYOROKU

THE GAY WATERWHEEL
   IN THE VALLEY
    POURS PETALS
FROM MOUNTAIN CHERRIES
CHOGETSU

Summer

O SPRINGTIME TWILIGHT...
   PRECIOUS MOMENT
   WORTH TO ME
A THOUSAND PIECES
                SOTOBA

REPLY:

O SUMMER TWILIGHT...
   BUG-DEPRECIATED
   TO A
MERE FIVE HUNDRED
                KIKAKU

BOUNCING BAMBOO DIPPER
   IN THE WATER-TUB...
   FOLLOWING
A FLY-AWAY BIRD
                HORO

A BABY SPARROW...
   HOPPING
   WITH CURIOSITY
TO WATCH MY BRUSHWORK
                  SHOHA

HOW COOL ... SWEET GRASSES
   SCYTHED IN FIELDS
   AT EARLY DAWN
ENTERING OUR GATE
                  BONCHO

ON THE GIDDY SWING...
   TINY GIRL-CHILD
   CLUTCHING TIGHT
HER SPRAY OF BLOSSOMS
                  ISSA

AH ROADSIDE SCARECROW
   WE'VE HARDLY
   STARTED GABBING...
AND I HAVE TO GO
                  IZEN

19

PERHAPS THE VOICELESS
   WANDERER DREAMS
   OF FLOWERS...
BUTTERFLY DOZER
          REIKAN

SOMETIMES THE FARMER
   TROTS OUT TO SEE
   HIS SCARECROW...
SLOWLY HE WALKS BACK
          BUSON

THAT DARK WATERFOWL
   ALTHOUGH APPEARING
   WEIGHTED...
SEE HOW IT CAN FLOAT!
          ONITSURA

AH BOLD NIGHTINGALE...
   EVEN BEFORE
   HIS LORDSHIP
YOU DON'T MEND YOUR SONG
          ISSA

20

THAT FAT OLD BULL-FROG
   SAT THERE STARING
   BACK AT ME
WITH A SOUR FACE
            ISSA

IN FLAT SUNSET LIGHT
   A BUTTERFLY
   WANDERING
DOWN THE CITY STREET
            KIKAKU

SOMEONE IS WALKING
   OVER THE WOODEN
   BRIDGE ... HEAR
THE DEEP FROG-SILENCE
            RYOTO

A WAGON RUMBLING ...
   AND OUT FROM
   SILENT GRASSES
A SUDDEN BUTTERFLY
            SHOHA

INTO THE BLINDING
   SETTING SUN THE
   SCARECROW STARES ...
STILL DIFFERENT

SHIRAO

GAY ... AFFECTIONATE ...
   WHEN I'M REBORN
   I PRAY TO BE A
WHITE-WING BUTTERFLY

ISSA

SQUATTING LIKE BUDDHA:
   BUT BITTEN
   BY MOSQUITOES
IN MY NIRVANA

OEMARU

AT THE ANCIENT SHRINE
   TARNISHED GOLD-FOIL ...
   AND GREEN LEAVES
AWAKENING TIME

CHORA

22

EVEN WITH INSECTS...
    SOME ARE HATCHED
    OUT MUSICAL...
SOME, ALAS, TONE-DEAF
                    ISSA

PLANTED ROWS OF BEANS
    AND RANDOM CLUMPS
    OF LILIES...
PROSPEROUS ISLET!
                    SHIKI

NIGHTINGALE WEEPING
    AND CEASELESS OCEAN
    MOANING...
SOON O SOON THE DAWN
                    SHIRAO

IN SUMMER MOONLIGHT...
    GLITTERING BROOKLET
    RUNNING
DOWN OUR VILLAGE STREET
                    SHIRAO

23

TWO JADE-GREEN HILLTOPS
  STAND IN THEIR
  SUMMER LEAFAGE
MIRROR-IMAGES
         KYORAI

YELLOW FIREFLY...
  LITTLE LAMP-FLAME
  THAT TO THE
HUMAN TOUCH IS CHILL
         SHIKI

SUNNY FIELDS AND WARM...
  SEE THE MONK'S FACE
  PEEPING OUT
FROM THE TEMPLE FENCE
         ISSA

A CRABLET CRAWLING
  UP MY ANKLE-BONE...
  AH COOL
MEANDERING BROOK
         BASHO

24

IN MY NATIVE PLACE
   THERE'S THIS PLANT:
   AS PLAIN AS GRASS
BUT BLOOMS LIKE HEAVEN
         ISSA

PITIFUL BLIND CHILD...
   AND SO BRIEF
   THE ROSE OF SHARON
GARLANDING HER PORCH
         SHIRAO

DAYLIGHT AT THE INN...
   THROUGH MY LOOPED
   MOSQUITO NETS
A MORNING-GLORY
         SHIRO

TWILIGHT WATERING...
   AND PLEASE,
   A COOLING SPRINKLE
FOR WRENS AND CRICKETS
         KIKAKU

25

HAVING TUMBLED OFF
    HIS GRASS-BLADE...
    THE FIREFLY
BUZZES UP AGAIN

BASHO

MOONLIGHT NIGHTINGALE
    CASTS A WHISTLING
    LINE OF SOUND
OVER THE MILLPOND

BASHO

AS LIGHTNING FLASHES...
    ZIG-ZAG SCREECHES
    OF THE HERON
FLYING IN THE DARK

BASHO

HEREBY I ASSIGN,
    IN PERPETUITY,
    TO WIT:
TO THIS WREN THIS FENCE

ISSA

STUBBORN WOODPECKER...
  STILL HAMMERING
    AT TWILIGHT
AT THAT SINGLE SPOT
          ISSA

AT SILENT NOONTIDE...
  FAR ACROSS
    THE FLOWER-FIELDS
HEAR THE SIGHING SEA
          BUSON

HEAR THE HUMMING
  OF HONEYSUCKLE
    PETALS FALL...
DISTURBED MOSQUITOES
          BUSON

THE SICKLY ORCHID
  THAT I TENDED SO...
    AT LAST
THANKS ME WITH A BUD
          TAIGI

POT-IMPRISONED NOW...
   PALELY DREAMING
     OCTOPUS
IN SUMMER MOONLIGHT
              BASHO

CURLED ON THE FAN...
   AHA! I'VE CAUGHT YOU
     TOM-CAT
FAST ASLEEP AGAIN!
              ISSA

HIGH SUN STILL BURNING
   IN THE FALCON'S
     EYES... DOWN TO
MY EARTH-BOUND WRIST
              TAIRA

BUT SEE THE MOUNTAIN...
   SHAKING WITH THE
     WAVES OF HEAT
WHERE DAY HAS GONE
             ONITSURA

28

WHAT A MONSTER KITE!
  EVEN THE BRAVEST
  EAGLE
WOULD NOT DARE ATTACK!
             SHIKI

YELLOW BUTTERFLY...
  FLUTTERING
  FLUTTERING ON
OVER THE OCEAN
            SHIKI

COOL ON BLUE WATER
  THAT OVERHANGING
  ISLET
WITH ITS PINE ASKEW
            SHIKI

WHAT A COOLING BREEZE!
  NOW ALL STIFLED
  GRASSHOPPERS
GAILY SING AGAIN
            ISSA

I WILL NOT FORGET
  THIS LONELY SAVOR
  OF MY LIFE'S
ONE LITTLE DEWDROP

BASHO

MOONLIGHT SLANTING
  THROUGH ALL THE
  BAMBOO FOREST...
AND NIGHTINGALE SONG

BASHO

IN THE RAIN-PINKED POND
  STILL-UNSLAUGHTERED
  SILLY DUCKS
REJOICE WITH QUACKING

ISSA

SPARROW FAMILY...
  PLAYING AT HIDE
  AND SEEK
IN THE TEA-BUSHES

ISSA

30

TWILIGHT FLOWER-FIELD...
   MOONRISE IN
   THE EASTERN SKY
SUNSET IN THE WEST
               BUSON

NIGHT IS DARKENING...
   SILENT IN
   THE PADDY POOL
SHINES THE MILKY WAY
               IZEN

ON THAT INCH OF LAND
   BEANS GREW TO
   OUR VERY DOOR...
YET GRAND IN MOONLIGHT!
               ISSA

WITH ME ON THE CLIFF
   ANOTHER POET...
   FELLOW-GUEST
OF THE SUMMER MOON
             KYORAI

INQUIRING WREN
  LOOKING HERE AND
  LOOKING THERE ...
HAVE YOU LOST YOUR BAG?
                ISSA

THE SADNESS OF IT ...
  UNDER THE
  HERO'S HELMET,
TARNISHED NOW, A CRICKET
                BASHO

TWO WATER-LILIES
  SHINING SERENELY
  GOLDEN ...
RAINDROP-DIMPLED POOL
                BUSON

WHILE THE BOBOLINK
  SINGS CHEERILY
  HE GIVES MY SHACK
THE COLD CRITIC'S EYE
                ISSA

FLOATING BUTTERFLY
   WHEN YOU DANCE
     BEFORE MY EYES . . .
ISSA, MAN OF MUD

         ISSA

SUPERNATURAL
   COOL BREEZE . . .
     BUDDHA'S PARADISE
MUST LIE THATAWAY

         ISSA

INSECTS POOR INSECTS . . .
   HOW WISE TO PURGE
     YOUR KARMA
CRYING PENITENCE

         OTOKUNI

WE HARK TO CRICKET
   AND TO HUMAN
     CHIRPINGS . . . WITH
EARS SO DIFFERENT

         WAFU

SLOW HOT SILENT HOURS ...
   IN THE AFTERNOON
   A PHEASANT
SETTLES ON THE BRIDGE
               BUSON

THE SOFT SUMMER MOON ...
   WHO IS IT MOVES
   IN WHITE THERE ...
ON THE OTHER BANK?
               CHORA

AT MY HUT I FEAR
   ALL I CAN REALLY
   TEMPT YOU WITH ...
SMALLISH MOSQUITOES
               BASHO

WHILE I SWOOP MY NET
   DELIBERATE
   BUTTERFLY
YOU NEVER HURRY
               GARAKU

AH . . . MORNING-GLORY
   GLOWING WITH
    THE INDIGO
OF SOME MOUNTAIN POOL
              BUSON

SILENT THE GARDEN
   WHERE THE
    CAMELLIA-TREE
OPENS ITS WHITENESS
            ONITSURA

FROM THE DAY IT'S BORN
   OF ABANDONED
    STICKS AND RAGS . . .
ELDERLY SCARECROW
            NYOFU

NOW THIS GOOD SEA-SLUG
   HAS BOTH HEAD
    AND TAIL . . . BUT GOD
KNOWS WHICH IS WHICH
            KYORAI

THAT NIGHT WHEN I HAD
    SOLD MY LOWER
    FIELD...I LAY
WAKEFUL FROM FROG-CALLS
          HOKUSHI

HEY! WHY DON'T YOU HELP
    THAT BUZZING
    HORSE-FLY OPEN
THE STICKING SKYLIGHT?
          ISSA

DAWN-TWITTERING BIRDS...
    OUR OVERNIGHT
    BIG-CITY GUEST
ALONE IS STIRRING
          SHOHA

TENDER BAMBOO-SHOOTS
    AND BABY'S TENDER
    GUM-PINKS...
TINY TOOTH-CUTTING
          RANSETSU

BOUNCING THE BALL...
    SHE BENDS TO MAKE
        A FACE AT HER
MEOWING KITTEN
                    ISSA

IN THE SUDDEN BURST
    OF SUMMER RAIN...
        WIND-BLOWN BIRDS
CLUTCHING AT GRASSES
                    BUSON

LIKE A BUTTERFLY...
    THE PILGRIM'S
        TOMBOY YOUNGSTER
TROTS UNEVENLY
                    SHIKI

THE MONKS EXHIBIT
    BUDDHA'S IMAGE...
        SPARROWS TOO
ARE DAWN-LIGHT LOOKERS
                    ISSA

37

Autumn

ON THE EBB-TIDE BEACH
   THE HURRYING CRAB
   STOPS SHORT...
THERE IS A FOOTPRINT!

          ROFU

BRACED IN THE WATERS...
   SCARECROW IN
   THE FLOODED FIELD
GRIMLY ENDURES IT

          SHIKI

AH MY FOREST HUT...
   WHERE THE FRIENDLY
   WOODPECKER
KNOCKS AT DOOR AND POST

          BASHO

ON THIS STILL WATER
   SEE WHERE
   HIS REFLECTION
MEETS THE WATERFOWL
                MAHARA

QUITE THE STUPIDEST
   OF ALL LIVING
   CREATURES IS
A DRY OLD SCARECROW
                SHIKI

AUTUMN NIGHTS ARE COLD...
   CRUSHING THE TINY
   CHILD TO ME . . .
WARM LOVELY YOUNGLING
                SHIKI

BEHIND THE TWISTED
   BRANCHES WITH
   THE EAGLE'S NEST...
RED SINKING SUN-BALL
                BONCHO

39

AS I LIGHT THE LAMP
    BEHOLD . . . TO EVERY
    SINGLE DOLL
ITS OWN REAL SHADOW
                        SHIKI

MOTHER LOST, LONG GONE . . .
    AT THE DEEP DARK SEA
    I STARE . . .
AT THE DEEP DARK SEA
                        ISSA

AH SACRED SWALLOW . . .
    TWITTERING OUT
    FROM YOUR NEST IN
GREAT BUDDHA'S NOSTRIL
                        ISSA

TEA-KETTLE HANDLE . . .
    I'LL CUT IT FROM
    THE BAMBOO
OF THAT BUBBLING WREN
                        KIKAKU

WEEPING...WILLOWS
KNEEL HERE BY
THE WATERSIDE
MINGLING LONG GREEN HAIR
KYORAI

GATHERING STARLINGS
CRY AS THEY
SPRINKLE BERRIES
FROM THE AUTUMN TREE
SHIKI

SILVERY HERRINGS
POURING...
A LIVE WATERFALL
FROM NET TO BASKET
KIKAKU

AH LEAFLESS WILLOW...
BENDING OVER
THE DRY POOL
OF STRANDED BOULDERS
BUSON

41

O YOU SNUB-NOSE DOLL!
  MAYBE YOUR
  MOTHER DIDN'T
PINCH AND PULL ENOUGH
            BUSON

PERCHED ON THE BAMBOO
  MARKER OF A
  NEW-DUG GRAVE...
THE WAITING DRAGONFLY
            KITO

ALL ALONG THE BEACH...
  PLOVERS PLAYING
  AT SOME GAME
INVOLVING WET-FOOT
            BUSON

WITH PHILOSOPHY
  HE CONTEMPLATES
  THE MOUNTAIN...
OLD PROFESSOR FROG
            ISSA

42

AT THE SETTING SUN...
   WASHING DOWN
   HIS WEARY HORSE
IN THE AUTUMN SEA
           SHIKI

ON THIS PLAIN OF MIST
   NOTHING BUT FLAT
   ENDLESSNESS...
AND RED-RISING SUN
          SHIRO

RISING HARVEST MOON...
   FROM THIS HUT
   AS YET UNWALLED
I WILL VIEW IT WELL
          SHIRAO

BITTER BROKEN REEDS...
   DAY IN DAY OUT
   THE FALLEN
FLOAT AWAY... AFAR
          RANKO

PENETRATING HOT
   SEPTEMBER SUN...
   ON MY SKIN
FEEL THE COOLING BREEZE
          BASHO

I AM GROWING OLD...
   O SWEET BIRD
   DISAPPEARING
INTO AUTUMN DUSK
          BASHO

WHO IS THAT, HUDDLED
   IN A STRAW-COAT...
   STARING AT OUR
HOLIDAY PARADE?
          BASHO

SEE THIS DRAGONFLY...
   HIS FACE IS
   PRACTICALLY
NOTHING ELSE BUT EYES
          CHISOKU

COMPANION CUCKOO...
    KEEP YOUR EYE COCKED
    ON MY HUT
UNTIL I COME BACK
                                ISSA

REDDISH MORNING SKY...
    RAIN FOR YOU TODAY
    I GUESS,
LITTLE LUCKY SNAIL!
                                ISSA

WITHIN PALE SILENCE
    SPREADING FROM
    EVENING MOONLIGHT...
SUDDEN CICADA
                                HAJIN

WET MORNING GARDEN...
    MY SUNNY
    CHRYSANTHEMUMS
ARE SEA-MIST-SHROUDED
                                SAMPU

45

WITH THE MOON-RISING...
  LEAF AFTER LEAF
  AFTER LEAF
FALLS FLUTTERING DOWN
            SHIKI

I DIDN'T ENTER...
  BUT I STOPPED
  IN REVERENCE...
AUTUMN-LEAF TEMPLE
            BUSON

SUDDEN RADIANCE...
  AFTER OCTOBER
  RAINSTORM
RE-REDDENED PEPPERS
            BUSON

THE PEOPLE, WE KNOW...
  BUT THESE DAYS
  EVEN SCARECROWS
DO NOT STAND UPRIGHT
            ISSA

ONLY WITHERED GRASSES
  IN YOUR CAGE?...
    O CRICKET CAPTIVE
MY APOLOGIES!

SHOHA

FROM FISH-BOAT TORCHES
  SPARKS ARE FALLING...
    POOR TETHERED
SCORCH-FACE CORMORANTS

KAKEI

THIS IS MY OWN PLACE...
  MUD-HUT AND
    COMPANION TREE
SHEDDING AUTUMN LEAVES

CHORA

FROM THE HAUNTED HUT
  SMOKE IS SEEPING
    IN THE RAIN...
SOMEONE IS INSIDE!

BUSON

SEPTEMBER LIGHTNING...
   WHITE CALLIGRAPHY
      ON HIGH
SILHOUETTES THE HILL
                    JOSO

SEE...SIX GAPING BEAKS
   WAITING FOR
      THE MOTHER-BIRD
IN COLD AUTUMN RAIN
                    ISSA

SILENT AUTUMN AIR...
   HERE AND THERE
      AMONG THE HILLS
RISING THIN BLUE SMOKES
                    GYODAI

THE FISHERMAN'S HUT...
   WHERE LIVELY CRICKETS
      MINGLE NOW
WITH DRYING SHRIMP
                    BASHO

48

RISING AUTUMN MOON...
   LIGHTING IN MY
   LAP THIS YEAR
NO PALE SICKLY CHILD
            ONITSURA

FOR FALL FESTIVALS
   OUR RELIGIOUS
   DRAGONFLIES
DON RED GARMENTS TOO
            ISSA

WILD GEESE O WILD GEESE
   WERE YOU LITTLE
   FELLOWS TOO...WHEN
YOU FLEW FROM HOME?
            ISSA

BY ABANDONED ROADS
   THIS LONELY
   POET MARCHES
INTO AUTUMN DUSK
            BASHO

49

Winter

TELL ME: WHERE DOES THIS
UNEXPECTED COLD SNAP
COME FROM . . .
WEATHERWISE SCARECROW?
ISSA

WINE-DRINKING-WAKEFUL
ALL ALONE THAT
BITTER NIGHT
I STARTED AT SNOWFALL
BASHO

SNOW-ISOLATED . . .
ONCE MORE I PRESS
MY BACK AGAINST
MY THINKING-POST
BASHO

50

BACK TO MY HOME TOWN
   AND BURIAL
    IN MY HUT...
FIVE COLD FEET OF SNOW
           ISSA

WINTER WOODCUTTER...
   WHEN YOUR AXE CUTS
    HOME I SCENT
UNEXPECTED SPRING
           BUSON

MY OLD FATHER TOO
   LOOKED LONG ON THESE
    WHITE MOUNTAINS
THROUGH LONELY WINTERS
           ISSA

FEEBLE FEEBLE SUN...
   IT CAN SCARCELY
    STRETCH ACROSS
WINTER-WASTED FIELDS
           BAKUSUI

51

WINTER-SOLITARY...
  I FIND SOLACE
  IN THIS OLD
CHINESE-PAINTED PINE
                    BASHO

THE MOURNING FATHER
DEEP UNDER ASHES...
  BURNING CHARCOAL
  CHILLED NOW BY
HIS HISSING TEARS
                    BASHO

IN THE RAINY DAWN
  SEE WHERE I CREPT
  OUT OF BED...
HOLE IN THE BEDCLOTHES
                    JOSO

A MOUNTAIN HAMLET...
  UNDER THE GREAT
  WHITE SNOWDRIFT
A GURGLING BROOK
                    SHIKI

52

AT FREEZING MIDNIGHT
   HEAR THAT RAT
   GO RUMMAGING...
DIRTY KITCHEN DISHES
          BUSON

EVEN MY LAMP-LIGHT...
   HIBERNATING
   IN A FROZEN
WINTER-WHITE HALO
          YAHA

LAST NIGHT A SNOWFALL...
   TODAY CLEAR COBALT
   HEAVEN AND
WHITE-MANTLED PINES
          ROKA

A BITTER NIGHT...BUT
   LONG PRACTICE
   WITH COLD HUNGER
PERMITTED ME TO SLEEP
          IZEN

53

SOFT SNOWFLAKES SETTLE
   DOWN ON THESE
   UNSTIRRING DUCKS ...
A WORLD OF SILENCE
                    SHIKI

WET SNOW IS SWEEPING
   OVER THE RED-BERRY
   BUSH ...
TWO SPARROWS CHIRPING
                    SHIKI

OVER AND OVER
   FROM MY BED
   I ASK MY NURSE:
NOW, HOW DEEP THE SNOW?
                    SHIKI

AT THIS DREARY INN
   A HOUND KEEPS
   WAILING ... LIKE ME
LONELY IN THE RAIN?
                    BASHO

54

THE VERY PLANETS
    GLEAMING THROUGH
    ITS SILHOUETTE...
FROZEN WILLOW-TREE
                        CHORA

EVERY SINGLE STAR
    IS QUIVERING NOW
    WITH LIGHT...
O HOW BITTER COLD
                        TAIGI

BRIGHT SOUL OF WINTER...
    MOONLIGHT
    PUNCTUATED BY
PATTERING HAILSTONES
                        GYODAI

BITTER WINTER WIND...
    WON'T IT BLOW
    RIGHT OFF THE SKY
THAT DAY-OLD CRESCENT?
                        KAKEI

55

NOW AT DAWN THE TIDE
  FLOATS INCOMING
  LAYERS ON
OUR NIGHT-FROZEN COVE
          SHIKI

POLISHING THE BUDDHA...
  AND WHY NOT
  MY PIPE AS WELL
FOR THE HOLIDAY?
          ISSA

ON A RAINY DAY
  THE DRIPPING
  SCARECROWS SEEM LIKE
ORDINARY MEN
          SEIBI

REMEMBERING
  THEIR PAINTED FACES...
  SHE UNWRAPPED
HER OLD PAIR OF DOLLS
          BUSON

IT IS WARM TODAY...
  BUT I THINK
  I FEEL THE CHILL
OF THAT WINTER SUN
                ONITSURA

CHILDREN, COME ON OUT:
  PATTERING
  ALONG THE LANE
SEE...IT'S HAILING PEARLS
                BASHO

ICY WATER NIGHT...
  I UNFREEZE
  THE WRITING-BRUSH
WITH MY TWO GOOD TEETH
                BUSON

OUT OVER THE LAKE
  LONG COLD
  HOLLOW EMPTINESS...
A SOLITARY CROW
                SHIKI

THOSE TWO TIRED DOLLS
   IN THE CORNER
     THERE ... AH YES,
THEY ARE MAN AND WIFE
ISSA

SILLY HAILSTONES ...
   FLEEING INTO
     MY FIREPLACE
FAST AS THEY CAN RUN
ISSA

IN ICY MOONLIGHT
   PIN-POINT-PATTERING
     PEBBLES
CRUNCHING UNDERFOOT
BUSON

COLD WINTER RAIN-LINES
   ARE LIFTED
     HORIZONTAL
BY THE HOWLING GALE
KYORAI

WITH HIS HAT BLOWN OFF
    THE STIFF-NECKED
    SCARECROW STANDS HERE
QUITE DISCOMFITED
                        BUSON

ICY-WINTER NIGHT...
    PERHAPS THE WATER-
    BIRDS, LIKE ME,
ARE LAKESIDE HUDDLERS
                        ROTSU

DARKENING SNOW-CLOUDS...
    OVER THIS WAITING
    LAKE AND LAND
BLACK BIRDS WHIMPERING
                        OTOKUNI

BLUE-SHADOW-BOLTED...
    THE CASTLE GATE
    OF EDO
IN FROZEN MOONLIGHT
                        KIKAKU

MY NEIGHBORS HATE ME...
  HEAR THEM BANG
  AND RATTLE PANS
IN THE ICY NIGHT

BUSON

THAT SNOTTY URCHIN
  LEFT UNPICKED
  BY EITHER TEAM...
AH THE BITTER COLD!

SHIKI

BEFORE THE BUDDHA
  EVEN GOOD SPARROWS
  BOW...PARENTS
AND CHILDREN BOTH

ISSA

A HARSH-RASPING SAW...
  MUSIC OF
  COLD POVERTY
IN WINTER MIDNIGHT

BUSON

60

YEAR-END REVELLING...
　　STILL IN PILGRIM'S
　　CAPE MUST I
ROAM MY ENDLESS ROAD
　　　　　　　BASHO

SINCE DEAR BASHO DIED
　　WHAT POEM-MAKER
　　DARES TO WRITE
"YEAR-END REVELLING"?
　　　　　　　BUSON

DEATH-SONG

I WAS ALLOTTED
　　TWO AUTUMNS MORE
　　THAN AVERAGE MAN
THE HARVEST MOON
　　　　　　　SAIKAKU

DEATH-SONG

ON THE LAST LONG ROAD
　　WHEN I FALL AND
　　FAIL TO RISE...
I'LL BED WITH FLOWERS
　　　　　　　SORA